WHAT EVERY MAN
NEEDS TO KNOW

WHAT EVERY MAN NEEDS TO KNOW

ROBERT PASICK

HarperSanFrancisco
A Division of HarperCollins*Publishers*

FIRST EDITION

Library of Congress Cataloging-in-Publication Data

Pasick, Robert S.

    What every man needs to know / Robert Pasick. — 1st ed.

      p. cm.

    ISBN 0-06-251064-9 (pbk. : alk. paper)

    1. Men—Conduct of life.   2. Middle-aged men—Conduct of life.   I. Title.

    BJ1601.P375 1994

    170'.81—dc20   94-4423

94 95 96 97 98 ❖ CWI 10 9 8 7 6 5 4 3 2 1

To the guys in the groups.
Thanks for your trust and
your wisdom.

Thanks to Chris Pearson
for all her many contributions.
Thanks to Patricia, Daniel, and Adam
for their support and great ideas.

These ideas are meant as beginning steps for men who want to make changes in key areas of their lives: relationships with women, children, other men, parents, and siblings; their understanding of their emotions, sexuality, and spirituality; their relationship to work, money, their bodies, and the community where they live. If you have ever felt old in your bones or weighted down by obligation or wanted to redefine and reinvent yourself, then you might find something useful here.

Please don't try to follow all 365 of the suggestions or you'll feel overwhelmed, which is the opposite of the intended effect. These are the ramblings of a white, mid-forties male from the Midwest who has had the opportunity to learn a lot from the men with whom he has worked. I wish to be helpful, and to make a difference for people who are seeking a better way to live.

This is not meant as a "self" help book. In fact, I believe that the notion that people can change all by themselves is misguided. *Most* change occurs when two or more people cooperate together. This is why the most successful behavior change programs (Alcoholics Anonymous, Weight Watchers, etc.) rely on group support as the primary structure for change. Throughout the book, I encourage men to work with other men in their effort to make significant changes in their lives.

Perhaps after reading this book you'll find yourself thinking more consciously about doing good deeds, about slowing down, about showing a little tenderness, about taking a walk in the woods with your dad, your daughter, your dog, or even by yourself. That would be nice. I hope to be doing the same.

WHAT EVERY MAN
NEEDS TO KNOW

1) Be radical and take off your tie.

2) Keep track of the daily abundances in your life.

   Focus on the positive; learn to appreciate what you have and tend to take for granted; avoid dwelling on problems, deficits, and worries.

3) If your work conflicts with your values, consider a career change.

4) Tell people when your feelings are hurt.

5) Call a relative or old friend you have lost touch with.

6) Learn to cook one great dish for every meal.

7) Arrange for a day to take your child to work with you.

8) Find a sacred place or a serene spot where you can retreat.

9) Let your wildness out by going out into the wilderness.

10) Acknowledge the power of your private demons.

All human beings experience fear, shame, and guilt.
Denying their existence only gives them more power.

11) Find out what it is in life you really enjoy doing and
do it!

12) Ask your mother about her experiences growing up as a young woman.

Getting to know your mother better will help you in your relationship with her, and in your relationship with other women. Take her to lunch and ask her to tell you stories about her life.

◆   ◆   ◆

13) Praise your mate in front of your children.

14) Keep a list of friends to call to have fun with or to talk over problems.

15) Play.

16) Practice harmony with the earth and all that live on it, including yourself.

17) Ask yourself why you are afraid to show (or express directly) love to other men.

18) It's never too late to make amends.

Ultimately, I believe we each know in our own hearts whether we have ever been abused or have abused someone else. As a first step, acknowledge those episodes to yourself. Then consider ways you might make amends for any acts of abuse you may have committed.

19) Play catch with your sons and daughters.

20) It takes two to decide the conversation is over.

21) If you spot a deer, keep watching it until it stops
watching you.

◆   ◆   ◆

22) In your daily calendar or journal, record activities that are nurturing: exercise, meditation, napping, calling a friend, or whatever you consider self-caring.

23) If you've been clean shaven, grow some hair. If you've always had hair, shave. Shake things up.

24) Love requires time; love requires courage.

25) Heal your relationship with your father.

26) Be sure to have fun with your loved ones.

27) Practice trusting other men.

Start one man at a time; find one man you can trust and confide in him.

28) Watch a thunderstorm with your mate or your children.

29) Interview your children about what it has been like to have you as a father.

30) Display a memento from your father or grandfather.

Search for something you have that your father and/or grandfather gave you. If you have nothing, ask for something (a watch, ring, photo, tool, cup, and so on) that he owned. Put it on display on your desk, toolbench, or dresser.

31) Put an equal amount of energy into your marriage as into your career.

32) Call at least one male friend a week.

33) Recognize your right (and responsibility) to feel good about yourself.

34) Learn a new sport.

35) Be clear and positive about your competencies.

Too often we learn to focus on our deficits and inadequacies. Living in a competitive environment, we compare ourselves to those above us on the ladder. Start a list of the skills you know you do well. Add to the list whenever you recognize another one.

36) For one week, don't tell people what to do.

37) Recognize that there are times in life when we cannot fix or help the ones we love.

38) Be kind and affectionate to your mate without expecting it to turn into intercourse.

39) Learn to say "thank you" to all compliments, even backhanded ones.

40) Write your own prayer.

Many men long for spirituality but reject organized religion. Yet they sense a spiritual practice could greatly enhance their lives. Start each day saying what you are thankful for; then build upon it to construct a prayer that makes sense for you.

41) Set reasonable expectations for your time by not biting off more than you can chew.

42) Generally, asking good questions is more productive than trying to come up with all the right answers.

43) Choose being happy over being right.

44) Find ways to mentor young men in your community or at work.

◆　　◆　　◆

45) With your mate, sit down and invent the future.

If you do not have a vision of where you want to be in the future, you will drift aimlessly toward a future you may not want. Plan a weekend retreat with your mate and envision the future.

46) Teach your children about your hobbies by letting them participate.

47) Seek sunrises and sunsets.

48) Learn yoga.

49) Learn to be more empathetic.

◆   ◆   ◆

50) It's never too late to mourn, even very old losses.

Develop meaningful rituals for loss. Examples of rituals include walking alone, sitting in church, meditating, writing in your journal, visiting with a trusted friend, planning a memorial service, and making a contribution in honor of the lost one.

51) You are not responsible for your parents' happiness.

52) Plan a romantic retreat with your partner (and make all the arrangements, including child care).

53) Organize a recycling program for your home.

54) Appreciate good ideas, wherever you find them.

55) Do not lie to your children, even a little.

56) Do not divide the world into winners and losers.

57) Show a little tenderness.

58) Allow yourself to contemplate during the day what it is that strikes terror into you at the fall of night.

◆   ◆   ◆

59) Make a column for "Family/Home" on your To-Do list.

Remember to keep your priorities balanced. Avoid becoming so preoccupied with work that you neglect your relationships with your mate and children and forget to do your "home" work. Every time you make a To-Do list, be sure to include items under "Family/Home."

60) Reach out to a friend in need.

61) Seek first to understand, then to be understood.

62) Go fly a kite.

63) Take the time away from work that you need to meet family obligations.

64) If you sense conflict growing, try to discuss it before it explodes.

65) Try something different sexually (not someone).

66) Take responsibility for your personal struggles so as not to transfer them to your children.

◆　　◆　　◆

67) Be aware of song lyrics floating in your mind.

Pop songs are the people's poetry. The songs you hum are a key to tuning into your emotions. When you hear a lyric in your head, listen to it, and ask yourself what it tells you about how you are feeling.

68) Get off the coffee/alcohol roller coaster.

69) Trust your feelings.

We have been taught to view feelings as a nuisance, an inconvenience, a sign of weakness, and something to be kept under control at all costs. Clinging to this view cuts us off from whole parts of ourselves: intuition, emotions, creativity. Talk to others about feelings or write them down.

70) If you lost a parent to death at an early age, reconnect with the lost parent's family (aunts, uncles, cousins, and so on) as a way to "find" the lost parent.

71) Give hugs when you leave and when you come home.

◆   ◆   ◆

72) Make a list of your personal guidelines for parenting.

Practice conscious parenting rather than reacting to your children based on your old learnings. Make a list of ten governing rules you want to follow as a parent, such as time with the children each day, discuss future plans for the children with your mate, and maintain consistency in discipline and household rules.

73) Cherish the past, live the moment, hope for the future.

74) Read books on new ways to bring sexual excitement into your relationship.

75) Ask yourself why you are afraid to cry, especially in front of other men.

76) Frame and display a picture of yourself as a happy child.

77) Spend one-on-one time with each of your parents.

It is crucial to get to know each parent on an individual basis in order to be able to free yourself of the pressure of family triangles. Each time you visit your parents, schedule alone-time with each of them. Talk to them separately on the phone, not in a three-way conversation.

◆　　◆　　◆

78) Plan an in-home getaway, when the children leave but you stay home alone.

79) Realize the joy you get from helping others.

80) Breathe deeply.

81) Take a dance class.

82) Evaluate how competitive you are.

Many of us thrive on competition. But it can seep into areas of our lives where we may not want it—in our relationships with our mates, our children, our friends. Take an honest look at how competitive you really are (in nonsport activities). Ask others. Move from competitive toward cooperative relationships.

83) Write down, in a secret place, one thing you will not talk about with anyone.

84) Talk with your parents about their hopes, fears, and wishes for their future.

◆   ◆   ◆

85) Identify and challenge your personal myths about sexuality.

Despite living through the sexual revolution, many of us remain confused about sex. In a Roper/Kinsey Institute poll only 10 percent of respondents correctly answered 80 percent or more of the items on "Fundamental Sexual Information." Read the *Kinsey Institute New Report on Sex* by June Reinisch and Ruth Beasley and take the test.

86) When someone has shared a painful story with you,
     follow up in a few days to see how he or she is doing.

87) Learn to overcome your fear of being thought of
     as unmanly.

     You can determine what is the right manhood for you,
     through intense self-exploration and having the courage
     to live as a man on your own terms.

88) Occasionally buy yourself a gift for a job well done.

89) Go to or organize a men's weekend retreat or
a men's group.

◆   ◆   ◆

90) Allow yourself to be sad.

We have been taught not to cry and to be "strong soldiers" in the face of loss. As a result, our grief has been short-circuited and adversely continues to affect our emotional development. Allow yourself to be sad and to cry and to reach out for support from a friend or loved one.

91) Ask your mate what she daydreams about. Then tell her about your daydreams.

92) Organize a reunion of your childhood or college friends.

93) Seek tranquillity in whatever you do.

94) You can handle the things you worry about.

Our monumental worries are often small potatoes in the larger scheme of life. Get in the habit of asking, What is the worst that could happen? Then ask the follow-up, What is the best? If the worst does happen, could I handle it?

95) Practice saying "I don't know" and "I'm not sure."

96) Pursue your artistic interests.

97) Write two separate letters to each of your parents: one expressing your gratitude and the other your disappointments.

These are not meant to be sent. They are to help you clarify your feelings. They should be written even if a parent is deceased.

98) To better understand women, read *The Dance of Anger* by Harriet Lerner.

99) Talk to other fathers about being a father.

Break the isolation from other men and get other male points of view about raising children. Start real conversations with the fathers of your children's friends about the challenge of fatherhood. Share your frustrations.

100) Live in ways that create, promote, and encourage peace of mind and peace on earth.

101) Have a place in your wallet where you keep a list of videos, music, or books that you want to buy or rent.

◆   ◆   ◆

102) Make your work environment a healthier place, physically and emotionally.

Don't just accept intolerable work conditions: poor lighting, dangerous toxins, abusive supervisors, long hours. Ask for what you need.

103) Be honest with yourself and with others.

104) Once in a while allow yourself to be one of the guys.

105) Do half of the housework.

She doesn't like doing dishes, washing, grocery shopping, and so on anymore than you do. You'll feel more like a part of the family if you make a commitment to take responsibility for at least half of the housework, and then remember to do it with excellence. By doing half, you can be twice the man you used to be.

106) Teach your children by what you do, not by what you say.

107) Simplify your life.

108) Use the one-day-at-a-time approach to change habits.

109) Buy a good set of tools.

110) Become more spiritual.

111) To understand yourself as a man, work on understand-ing your family dynamics and identifying your role in the family.

112) Spend time each night working *and* playing with your child.

113) Study and practice the Serenity Prayer:

> *God grant me Serenity*
> *To accept the things I cannot change,*
> *Courage to change the things I can, and*
> *Wisdom to know the difference.*

114) Learn to play a musical instrument.

115) Go a week without teasing.

116) Draw upon the right side of your brain.

We have been trained to worship the analytical,
logical way of thinking (the left-brain approach) and
to mistrust the more creative and intuitive thinking
style (the right-brain approach). In doing so, we deny
a crucial and elemental part of ourselves. Focus on
creativity and intuition for a day.

◆   ◆   ◆

117) Join with other men to protest excessive violence in society. Read *Men's Work: To Stop Male Violence* by Paul Kivel.

118) Cherish small victories and learn from small defeats.

119) Tell your children how proud you are of them and how proud they should be of themselves.

Your children crave your approval. Praise them often with warmth and sincerity.

120) Learn to savor solitude. Go away by yourself at least one weekend a year.

121) Relax.

   Learn to kick back. Spend some time in a hammock. Enjoy the day!

122) True or False? I am what I produce.

◆　　◆　　◆

123) When you apologize, do it twice: once in person
(or by phone) and once by letter.

To show the apology is sincere, be as persistent with
the apology as you are with getting what you want.

♦　　♦　　♦

124) Take an active stance in your community on behalf of children.

Do something to make the community a better place for children. Read the local paper, attend school board meetings, plan and build a playground in your neighborhood.

125) No matter how troublesome telling the truth might be, do not lie to your mate.

126) When wronged, learn to confront in a gentle manner.

127) Act on your dreams. Now.

128) Recognize that there's a lot in life we cannot fix.

129) Too much work can be hazardous to your family's health.

130) Learn to tell people what's bothering you.

131) If you have ever abandoned children, have the courage to find them and let them know you care.

◆　　　◆　　　◆

132) Share your background and needs with your mate.

A healthy relationship is based on mutual understanding. By keeping our feelings to ourselves, we create an unhealthy imbalance in our intimate relationships. Share your needs, even if you think they are silly or unimportant.

◆　　◆　　◆

133) Congratulate people on their success.

134) Try sleeping a little longer (by going to bed a little earlier).

135) Listen to your body when you experience pain.

136) If you fear homosexuals, ask yourself why.

137) Take the opportunity to show love.

Don't let life's little details fill up so much of your time that you never get around to showing your loved ones how much you care.

138) Make a commitment to your friends to talk it out when things are bothering any of you.

139) Accept your mate's right to say no.

140) Plan activities with other fathers and their children.

141) Learn the words to "Amazing Grace."

> *Amazing grace! How sweet the sound*
> *That saved a wretch like me!*
> *I once was lost, but now am found,*
> *Was blind, but now I see.*

◆　　　◆　　　◆

142) Make an adventure you have long dreamed of a reality.

Being responsible by making a living predominates our lives, somehow never leaving time for *adventure*. Do small adventures now; plan for big adventures by setting a goal date NOW, no matter how far in the future it may be. Plan it with a friend or your mate.

143) Learn to manage pain, anger, and shame without dumping on someone else.

144) Plan a block party.

Do something about the sense of isolation and alienation that has become so commonplace in our lives and in our neighborhoods. Contact a small group of neighbors to form an organizing committee for a block party. Take some leadership and be sure to follow through with details.

145) Identify and process vulnerable and tender emotions.

146) Tell your mate she's beautiful.

147) Go to your children's activities, even during
the workday.

Your children thrive on your support. Be there when
they perform, especially when it takes an extra effort.
They will appreciate it, even though they may not tell
you so.

148) When you walk, feel your feet make contact with the earth. When you love, feel your soul connect with the other human being.

◆　　◆　　◆

149) Are you a workaholic?

1. *Can you always justify working more?*
2. *Do you feel lost without work to do?*
3. *Are your friends, spouse, or children concerned that you work too much?*
4. *Do you worry that you work too much?*
5. *Can you exercise control over the amount of work you do for an extended period of time?*
6. *Do you hide from your problems by working more?*

7. *Do you boast of your exploits at work?*

8. *Can you imagine living without work? Would you work if you didn't need the money?*

9. *Do you feel you have a choice over how much you work?*

10. *Do you lie about how much you work?*

If you answered yes to more than five, you may be a workaholic. If so, take time off to reevaluate why you depend so much on work to feel okay about yourself.

150) Write down jokes you want to remember.

151) Strengthen your relationship with your siblings.

◆　　◆　　◆

152) Ask your mate about what it was like to grow up female.

A woman's experience growing up is very different from a man's. To be committed to a woman means actively seeking to understand her story. Ask her about her life and listen intently. Remember, do not try to rewrite her story.

153) Hug your children.

154) Make a list of your own personal stress busters.

We continually learn ways to combat stress, but in times of stress we forget them. Make a list of stress busters and keep it in your wallet. When you are stressed, pull it out and practice one or two of these methods.

155) Do one thing at a time.

156) Learn the difference between "being responsible" and "sticking your nose in other people's business."

157) Acknowledge to others that at times you feel vulnerable.

Recognize that admitting vulnerability can be a sign of newfound strength. Start by letting those you love and trust the most know that, at times, you feel scared, ashamed, or anxious.

158) As a way to work on forgiving your parents, remember that they, too, were once wounded children, like their parents before them.

159) The work of showing love is tougher than any job.

◆　　◆　　◆

160) Limit your school-age children's TV watching and video-game playing to the weekend (or for special events only).

Don't rely on TV to babysit and socialize your children rather than doing the work of childrearing yourself. Set up a rule and stick to it; use the VCR to tape if there is a show the children like during the week.

161) How has your concept of God changed from when you were a child?

162) Are you a Type A personality?

Three signs of Type A personality:

1. *A strong sense of time urgency—always fighting the clock.*
2. *Chronic activation—staying active, revved up, on the go most of the time.*
3. *Being multiphasic—constantly doing more than one thing at a time.*

People who are Type A personalities may be "hooked on their own hormones." Type As are at an increased risk for coronary heart disease.

◆   ◆   ◆

163) Dare to redefine what it means to be powerful as a man.

164) Read Susan Jeffers's book, *Feel the Fear and Do It Anyway*.

165) Have those important conversations with significant people in your life.

The things we are afraid to say may be more important than the daily jabber that fills our lives.

166) Without intercourse, pleasure each other to orgasm.

167) Be careful not to praise girls only for their looks and boys only for their actions.

◆   ◆   ◆

168) Learn to recognize the irrational beliefs that make you unhappy.

Most of us carry an irrational set of expectations about how we are supposed to perform and how the world is supposed to be. Trying to live up to these beliefs and expecting others to live up to them makes us miserable.

169) Join a sports league.

170) Appreciate how important your job is to you.
Learn to value your contribution at work.

171) Know when your children are old enough for you
to stop giving them money and advice.

172) Don't lose yourself in your relationship.

Remember to maintain balance. Recognize that you
do not need another to be a complete person. Keep
up other meaningful friendships with both men
and women.

173) Go out with your mate on an shopping spree and buy
each other undergarments.

174) Cultivate optimism about self, family, and the world.

175) Eat without reading.

176) Allow yourself to play the fool sometimes.

◆   ◆   ◆

177) When you feel the need to reclaim power and self-esteem, seek other avenues than aggression.

We have learned to see aggression as a legitimate means of gaining control over others. Yet, the expression of aggression hurts others and inevitably leads to a further deterioration of our self-esteem. Find new ways to feel powerful, or even go as far as to question your need to feel powerful.

178) Tell the story of your childhood to your children.

Include the mistakes and hard knocks as well as the victories.

179) When your partner is doing the pleasuring, lie back and be passive for a change.

◆   ◆   ◆

180) Contemplate death rather than running scared from the very thought of it. Write your own obituary, just as you wish it to be.

181) See beauty where others may have missed it.

Dew on a spider web . . . a child's smile . . . look around you.

182) To retain a sunny disposition: Get up every morning
and make a choice to be happy that day.

183) If you'll carry it, they will load more on.

184) Rise above it.

◆　　◆　　◆

185) Get involved in a project to improve the world.

Seek out an organization locally that represents some of your values. Think globally, act locally.

186) It's never too late to learn the art of making love.

◆   ◆   ◆

187) Remember to send birthday cards to your friends and family.

A friendship is strengthened by attentiveness. Write down the birth dates of friends and family in your appointment book (note a week before the birthday to send a card). Keep a supply of cards in your desk.

188) Continue the rituals and traditions of your ethnic group.

189) By clinging to what could have been, you "what-if" yourself to a slow death.

◆　　◆　　◆

190) Learn to say no, especially to more work demands on
your time.

The inability to say no stems from the need to please.
By never saying no we become overwhelmed by obligations. No time is left for caring for the soul. Try saying no for a month; never say yes until you allow
yourself to think it over.

191) Trust your feelings. You know more than you think you do.

192) Stand up for something or someone you care about.

◆　　◆　　◆

193) Rank in order the following three statements as you feel about them now:

   1. *I am proud of my relationship with my mate.*
   2. *I am proud of my relationship with my children.*
   3. *I am proud of my accomplishments at work.*

Now, rank them again as you would like them to be.

194) Ask your friends about their family histories.

195) Recognizing the limits of your knowledge is the beginning of wisdom.

196) If you let external pressures drive you, they will control your life.

◆　　◆　　◆

197) Grown men may not cry, but growing men do.

Reframe tears as a sign of strength rather than a sign of weakness. Learn to cry. First step: Give yourself permission.

198) Waking up emotionally is like having a whole box of tools and suddenly learning what they are all used for.

199) Develop a positive vision for yourself in old age.

200) Do something each day to show your mate you care.

201) Become involved in your children's schools.

Do you act as if school is a place to avoid rather than an important institution in your life? Be a volunteer in your child's classroom, join the PTA, take time off from work to go on a field trip or a school camping trip.

202) If you want to write, start writing; if you want to sail, start sailing; and so on.

203) Know when it's time to quit.

204) Security is not having a lot of money; it is knowing you can do without it.

205) Try your hand at poetry.

   For encouragement, read Robert Bly's *The Rag & Bone Shop of the Heart,* a book of poetry for men.

206) Ask yourself, "Whose burden am I carrying?"

207) Try all-day foreplay.

208) Be specific in your praise.

209) Live intentionally.

210) Learn to love your body.

211) Define for yourself what it means to "have balls."

We never define manhood on our own terms. Write down the term and define it for yourself. By this standard, do you have balls?

212) Start a garden.

213) Take up painting (or some form of art) as a way to relax without keeping score.

◆   ◆   ◆

214) Remember: Women are allies, not the enemy.

Media reports would lead us to believe we are embroiled in a war between the sexes. Yet, women's needs and men's needs are quite the same: to love and be loved, to be respected, to have the opportunity to be productive and not to be dominated. Together we may be able to move closer to these goals.

215) Allow freedom of speech in your own home.

216) Have a vision for the life you want to live and know who you want with you in that life.

217) Take a twenty-minute break every four hours.

218) Redefine wealth by counting the number of friends you have.

219) Plan a motel/hotel getaway.

220) Honor your heroes and your heroines.

Recognize and honor heroes in your family and in your local community.

221) Recognize and modify your need to be in control.

Stop trying to control all situations. "Going with the flow" is good for the heart and soul.

222) Write letters to your children.

223) Do one good deed each day for someone else. Do one good deed each day for yourself.

224) Do something just for *fun*.

225) Give proper due to those who have helped you get where you are today.

226) If you find yourself quick to anger, perhaps anger is masking other emotions you've learned to avoid expressing.

227) Have the courage to change dysfunctional family patterns.

If you understand your family history, you can better prevent repeating dysfunctional family patterns. In one way or another, all families have some dysfunction. The key is to understand both sides and to maximize the functionality in your family.

◆　　　◆　　　◆

228) Give your mate the time and space she needs to make the necessary changes in her life.

229) Teach your children about healthy sexuality.

Your children, especially your sons, look to you for information about sex. Begin by educating yourself.

230) Recognize, learn to control, and take full responsibility for your violent impulses.

231) Take action to resolve problems.

232) You are more than your career.

Whether we agree with this statement or not, too few of us act as if it were true. We devote our prime energy, the abundance of our time, and our primal passion to work. Make daily efforts to keep life in balance and work in its proper perspective.

233) Recognize there are loved ones we cannot fix or help.

234) There is a time when you can stop competing with your father.

235) Plan snuggle mornings.

Set out cereal for the children. Set up the coffeemaker in your room and put a Please Do Not Disturb sign on the door.

236) Fight for women's rights, including your daughter's rights.

237) Give thanks for the blessings of each day.

238) Learn how to set goals successfully.

239) You can only take others as far as you've gone yourself.

240) Warning: Anger may be harmful to your health.

Anger has its place. While it shouldn't always be repressed, learn the difference between appropriate and inappropriate ways of dealing with this emotion.

241) Thinking of having an affair? Think twice.

242) Avoid shaming young men or boys for not "being man enough."

243) Think carefully about what you are seeking.

Remember George Bernard Shaw's advice: "There are two tragedies in a man's life. One is the failure to get one's heart's desire; the other is getting it."

244) Rediscover the power of laughter.

Have you heard yourself have a hardy laugh lately? If the laughter has faded, maybe you're working too hard.

245) Caregiving is men's work, too.

246) Do what you can to alleviate the pain of others.

247) Use old photographs to encourage your parents to tell you about their family histories.

Tape-record their reminiscences about family history. Take your parent on a visit to his/her hometown and to the family cemetery. Listen carefully to his/her stories.

248) Remember, she fell in love with that kinder, sensitive side of you.

249) Keep commitments to friends and loved ones.

   If you tell someone you'll call, place the name on your business call-back list. Friends and loved ones are just as important as business associates.

250) Accentuate the positive.

251) Learn to hear your mate's criticism without responding defensively. Control your urge to criticize your mate in response.

252) Keep track of the number of hours you work each week.

To learn to work moderately and to keep life in better balance, keep track in your appointment book of the number of hours worked, including time spent working at home and time on the phone.

253) Find courage and strength in admitting you don't have it all together.

As Alice Walker says, "*Nobody* has it all together."

254) Read women's literature.

We are living in the midst of a major revolution about gender roles, yet we rely on newspapers or TV to help us understand it. We owe it to ourselves to try to learn firsthand about it. Ask women friends for recommendations.

255) Treat yourself as well as you treat your guests.

256) Redefine *courage* based on your own ideas about life and manhood.

257) Make a list of what you need in your life to maintain well-being and balance (such as eight hours sleep, playtime, daily walks with your mate, and so on).

258) Keep an even keel.

259) Ask yourself: Under what circumstances (if any) would you want your son or daughter to go to war?

If there is a difference, why?

260) Encourage the caring aspects of your son's personality.

261) Get used to going to the doctor for checkups.

Most men wait until a health problem is so severe that drastic intervention is required.

262) When you choose between two evils, you are still choosing an evil.

263) Charge into emotionally difficult conversations and finish them.

◆   ◆   ◆

264) On the anniversary of a family member's death, plan some type of mourning ritual.

Light a candle, play a song, write a poem, or whatever seems meaningful to you.

265) Respect your mate's standards for cleanliness and neatness.

266) After your children are old enough to leave home, give them a gift by leading a life independent of them.

267) Stop at all scenic view signs.

268) Look forward to old age as a time you can give up having to act tough. (Why not give it up before you get old?)

269) Be gentle on yourself.

270) Learn from your elders.

Get to know older men and women and seek
their wisdom.

◆   ◆   ◆

271) Ask daily how your mate is doing and listen intently to her answer.

She will really appreciate your interest in her life. Make it a habit. Don't read the newspaper or the mail or watch TV while listening to the answer.

272) Be more open and sharing in friendships, especially with other men.

273) Never argue with people who have to be right.

274) Women like men who like women.

275) It takes more strength to stop violence than to perpetuate it.

276) "Expressing your feelings" does not mean dumping on others.

277) Show affection to your mate in front of the children.

278) Encourage your son to be a good person, rather than a "good boy"; encourage your daughter to be a good person, rather than a "good girl."

279) Do your best and hope for the best outcome.

Recognize that once the dice are thrown, you cannot control how they will fall.

280) Find humor anywhere and everywhere.

Thirteen-year-old boys scan for humor. Learn to recultivate the thirteen-year-old humor seeker in you by noticing funny incidents in your life on a daily basis.

281) Do the tough stuff first, and reward yourself with fun stuff later.

282) Emotion is your body talking to you.

283) At the appropriate age, tell your children about your family secrets. If they remain secrets, they can become toxic to your family, too.

284) Don't take love for granted.

285) Get to know the parents of your children's friends.

286) Walk on the sunny side of the street.

287) Take some small risks each day.

288) Write an ideal job description for yourself.

Place it in your pocket notebook and look for and create opportunities to fill it.

289) Ask yourself before jumping in to solve a problem, Is it my problem, or is it someone else's problem?

290) Is being right ever more important than being
a friend?

291) Smile, especially at your mate and children.

As Thich Nhat Hanh says, "If in our daily lives we can
smile, we can be peaceful and happy. Not only we but
everyone will profit from it." He suggests remembering
to smile when you wake up. Use a cue—a picture, a
leaf—so you remember.

292) To understand your children better—without judging—listen to their favorite radio stations.

Remember what music meant to you as a child and how your parents reacted to it.

293) Make wishes (especially upon the evening's first star).

294) Develop an aerobic exercise routine.

295) You don't have to go it alone.

296) Be clear and positive about your skills.

Make a list of them to keep in your pocket notebook.
When you're feeling down, read them.

297) In relationships, trying to win all the battles inevitably
leads to losing the war.

298) Ask your mate what special favor she wishes for and then do exactly that.

299) Read parenting magazines. They're not for women only.

300) Become passionately interested in something entirely unrelated to your work.

301) Remember that well-being is something other than being well-off.

We falsely learn to believe that our happiness depends on how much money we have. Ask yourself if the happiest times of your life have been the times when you made the most money. Maybe your unhappiness is not about money.

302) Learn to challenge your internal critic.

303) To stay emotionally committed to someone is extremely difficult, but to be alone is impossible.

304) Challenge the "I'll be happy when . . . " myth.

Make up your mind to be happy here and now. Refuse to wait for one more success, as if magically with that next achievement happiness will appear.

305) Your marriage will work as well as you are determined to make it work.

But remember, it does take consistent effort and work.

306) Raise your children in a bullshit-free environment.

307) Ask others what they do to find peace of mind.

◆   ◆   ◆

308) Take a hike. If you walk far enough, you will leave your troubles behind.

309) Voice your disapproval when you hear a sexist joke.

Be an ally to women in the fight against sexism. It takes courage, at any age, to speak up. This goes for racist jokes, as well.

◆   ◆   ◆

310) Accept full responsibility for your behavior when you lose your temper.

311) Write personal notes of appreciation.

312) Touch with love. Learn the art of massage with your mate.

313) Find positive alternatives to physical punishment.

314) Remember the good in yourself, as well as in other people.

315) Learn from your mistakes.

316) Learn to say no (when you mean no), even if you think it will upset others.

317) Find profundity in people, whether they be rich or poor.

318) Develop a healthy morning routine. Get up early in the morning to write, walk, and/or meditate.

319) Tell her what pleases you, and what she does that you'd like more of.

320) Know why you fear the men you do and be aware of who fears you.

◆   ◆   ◆

321) Identify your key words to live by.

Some words I particularly like:

- *renew, reclaim, recreate*
- *meaningful, purposeful, useful*
- *spirit, energy, creativity*
- *ho-ho-ho, music, play, dance*
- *laughter, spontaneity, mirth*
- *connection, reconnection, forgiveness*
- *relational, sensational, sensual*
- *restore, revitalize, rejuvenate*

322) Three psychological benefits to regular exercise:

 1. *Reduce anxiety.*
 2. *Decrease the level of mild to moderate depression.*
 3. *Reduce stress.*

323) If you are having feelings for another woman, tell your mate.

◆   ◆   ◆

324) You can't solve emotional problems alone. Find strength
by reaching out to friends in your times of need.

325) In reviewing your life so far, pay attention to the times
when you have felt most useful in the world.

Strive to continue to search for ways to feel useful,
even indispensable to others.

326) Ask her what she enjoys about sex.

327) Know your areas of vulnerability as a parent.

We all have our parenting Achilles' heels: Is yours temper, impatience, indifference, or ignorance about children? Whatever it is, find it, identify it, and deal with it before it damages your relationship with your child.

328) Stop at park benches along the path.

329) Stand up to someone you are afraid of.

330) Set reasonable challenges for yourself: daily, weekly, yearly, and long-term.

When the mind isn't focused on a task, it tends to veer toward boredom or anxiety. Strive to set confronting challenges for yourself, but be sure to think of how these challenges impact others in your life.

331) Do what you need to do to be brave.

332) Your children are not yours alone; they belong to the world.

333) Alternate pleasing her and pleasing yourself.

Power issues can ruin a sexual relationship. Talk with your mate about power. One experiment is to take turns focusing completely on what she finds pleasurable and focusing exclusively on your pleasure.

334) Learn to ask for help.

335) Acknowledge hearing what your partner is saying.

336) Learn to focus solely on what you are doing at any one moment.

337) Be bigger than the next guy.

338) Do you fear a friendship might break under the weight of more intimacy?

We learn to keep friendships with other men on the "light" side, fearing that if we share too much about our fears or insecurities, the friend will reject us. Friendship can only grow with mutual self-revelation.

◆　　　◆　　　◆

339) Take a bike ride through your old neighborhood.

340) Respect is what she wants; respect is what she needs (and ditto for your children).

◆   ◆   ◆

341) Plan regular trips or outings with each of your children.

The best way to get close to your children is by spending one-on-one time, when they can receive your undivided attention and you can receive theirs. Plan trips well ahead of time. Bring a child on business trips or seize the moment and do spontaneous activities with him or her.

342) Practice forgiving yourself. Nobody is perfect. Acknowledge mistakes and move on.

343) While you may strive to live for a long time, also focus on staying alive in each moment.

◆   ◆   ◆

344) Recognize hidden signs of stress: irritability, headaches, body aches, tiredness, dry mouth, free-floating anxiety, stomach discomfort, sleep problems. We each have our own personal signs. Get to know them and when they occur, ask yourself, What is making me stressed-out?

345) More of our personality is determined by genetics and biology than we generally acknowledge.

346) Write thank-you notes.

   To let people know you appreciate them, buy some
   nice cards and keep them in your briefcase or in the
   car. When the spirit moves you, write a brief note
   of thanks.

347) Love's a game of give and take.

348) Recognize your personal blocks and obstacles to intimacy.

349) Make peace with yourself first.

350) Keep learning. It's never too late to go back to school and learn something new.

351) Learn to apply the skills that make you successful at
work to your life at home.

If you are creative at work, you can apply your
creativity to helping your children, planning meals,
organizing the kitchen, or planning social activities
with your friends.

◆   ◆   ◆

352) Escalating aggression only leads to more aggression.

It is a myth to believe we can ever impose control over others through aggression. It is merely a way of boosting your own fragile sense of manhood.

353) Expecting gratitude for a good deed inevitably leads to disappointment.

354) Keep the children out of disagreements with your mate.

355) Reconnect with long-lost friends.

Write a letter or call, stating that you miss the friend and would like to reconnect. Have courage: He may be so shocked to hear from you that at first he may seem unfriendly. Don't let this dissuade you; he's probably delighted to hear from you, even if he is a bit startled.

356) Set limits with friends and colleagues who take more than they give.

357) Challenge yourself to become a better listener.

358) Know what you do to put off other men.

We all know how to defend ourselves from other men. The challenge is to learn to take off our masks and to put down our swords and shields in the presence of men.

◆   ◆   ◆

359) Whom do you envy? Why?

360) Celebrate birthdays, including your own.

361) Learn the art of apology.

We learn that apology is an admission of error, yet we learn that making errors is terrible. Learn to apologize fully without adding a "but." Don't expect an apology in return.

362) You have the power to build your children's self-esteem but you can diminish it by trying to overcontrol them.

363) Find a task you can devote your life to.

◆　　　◆　　　◆

364) Keep a travel checklist in your wallet of what to bring, what to do before you leave, important numbers to call, and so on.

365) Be a man of your word.

◆　　　◆　　　◆

Rob S. Pasick, Ph.D., is the author of *Awakening from the Deep Sleep* and is coauthor of *Men In Therapy.* He is a psychologist, family therapist, and consultant at the Ann Arbor Center for the Family in Michigan. A graduate of Harvard University, he conducts workshops on gender issues in the workplace.